Britney Spears (2023 Revised and Analyzed)

ISBN 978-1-312-24514-3
Jonty Petty

TABLE OF CONTENT

CHAPTER 1

Early Life and Career

While Britney Jean Spears' birth certificate lists her place of birth as McComb, Mississippi, she really spent the most of her formative years in the Louisiana town of Kentwood. She has an elder brother named Bryan and was born to parents Lynne Irene Bridges and James Parnell Spears. Britney was raised with a blend of traditional Southern values and a passion for music by parents who had strong roots in their community.

Britney had a standard American upbringing in Kentwood. Lynne, her mother, taught elementary school, and James, her father, was a contractor. They reared their kids in a devout Baptist home where they could learn the importance of family and religion. Britney has always been interested in the stage, and particularly in singing and dancing.

Britney Spears always had an incredible gift for singing and performing. She began taking dancing lessons at the young age of three, and her parents saw immediate promise in her. She was a student at Parklane Academy, where she actively took part in several talent events and other extracurricular activities. As she performed her songs and dances for her loved ones, her passion for them only deepened.

When Britney was just eight years old, she tried out for "The Mickey Mouse Club," a talent competition program on the Disney Channel. But at the time, she was deemed too young for the program. But that just strengthened her resolve to work in the entertainment industry.

Britney Spears tried out for "The Mickey Mouse Club" again when she was 10 years old, despite having been rejected before. This time, her innate skill, charm, and stage presence were enough to attract the attention of the show's producers. As a member of "The Mickey Mouse Club," Britney joined the ranks of future megastars like Justin Timberlake, Christina Aguilera, and Ryan Gosling in 1992, when she was only 11 years old.

Britney's appearance on "The Mickey Mouse Club" was a huge boost in terms of exposing her talents to a broader audience. As a result of her work on the program, she received acclaim from viewers and respect from her peers in the entertainment world. Britney was one of the show's highlights because she displayed maturity and self-assurance beyond her years.

Britney returned to Kentwood after the show was canceled in 1994 and resumed her training as a performer. She dreamed of being a famous singer when she was in high school, so she entered talent shows around town.

Early exposure to the entertainment world via "The Mickey Mouse Club" was a pivotal milestone in Britney's rise to fame. It gave her a taste of stardom while also preparing her for the rigors of a career in the entertainment industry. She became a pop star because of the encouragement and inspiration she received from this encounter.

Britney Spears' humble beginnings in Kentwood and on "The Mickey Mouse Club" were crucial in setting the stage for her meteoric rise to fame and making her one of the most recognizable pop artists in history. Britney's path from aspiring pop singer in a tiny town to global icon was just getting started, and the world was about to witness the ascent of the Princess of Pop.

CHAPTER 2

Breakthrough and Rise to Stardom

Following her time on "The Mickey Mouse Club," Britney Spears moved back to her hometown of Kentwood with the intention of launching a music career. In 1997, her parents took a huge step when they drove Britney to New York City so she could audition for record companies, recognizing her enthusiasm and aptitude. She contacted many record companies, including Jive Records.

Britney Spears, at 15 years old, was signed to a recording deal by Jive Records after the label was impressed by her personality, skill, and promise. Her career as a music artist had officially began. The recording of her first album began in 1998, with the working title "Hit Me Baby One More Time."

After some time, though, the title was trimmed to "...Baby One More Time."

The debut song by Britney, "Baby One More Time," was released in January of 1999. The song's infectious pop tune and classic music video featuring schoolgirls helped it become an instant sensation. The song propelled Britney Spears to international popularity, topping charts across the world. The song achieved unparalleled popularity, launching her to instant worldwide renown.

Britney Spears' first studio album, "...Baby One More Time," was released on January 12, 1999. It became an international sensation, beloved by millions of people overnight. For fans of pop music, the album was an immediate classic because it perfectly captured Britney's young vitality, strong voice, and magnetic personality.

"Baby One More Time," the album's first single, marked the beginning of Britney's dominance in the pop music industry. Multiple successful singles were released from this album, including "Sometimes," "(You Drive Me) Crazy," and "From the Bottom of My Broken Heart." Britney's versatility as an artist was on full display throughout these tracks, further cementing her status as the new "Princess of Pop."

Britney's fast climb to prominence may be attributed in large part to her looks. Her mostly youthful fan following was won over by her relatable, girl-next-door persona, attractive dancing routines, and stylish sense of dress. Teenagers all around the world looked up to her and tried to copy her fashion choices, helping to elevate her to the level of cultural icon.

Britney Spears, when just 17, ruled the charts and made headlines throughout the world. The universal appeal of her music and the intensity of her live shows propelled her to international fame.

Britney Spears's ability to captivate her audience in both her music videos and her live performances was a major factor in her success. Her music videos became iconic, often serving as trendsetters and shaping the worlds of fashion and pop culture. Britney's appearance in a schoolgirl uniform in the now-iconic music video for "Baby One More Time" sparked discussions over propriety and cemented her reputation as a trailblazing performer.

After the success of her first album, Britney proceeded to deliver chart-topping songs accompanied by equally iconic music videos. Scenes from the movie "Drive Me Crazy" appeared in the music video for "(You Drive Me) Crazy," in which Britney had a brief appearance. The video featured her in several roles, not just singing, adding to her star power.

It came as no surprise that Britney's follow-up album, 2000's
Britney's burgeoning inventiveness and desire to experiment with visual storytelling were on full display in the album's music video for the title tune, which featured her as an astronaut on Mars.

Britney's live shows were just as exciting as her recordings. Her theatrical presence and planned dances were praised by reviewers. Her unforgettable performances at award ceremonies like the MTV Video Music Awards made her a household name, especially her rendition of "I'm a Slave 4 U" with a real snake.

As her early career progressed, Britney Spears became an icon of American popular culture. From billboards to magazine covers, her likeness was everywhere. Her influence on the entertainment business was unmistakable, and she became a fashion and style icon.

Finally, Britney Spears's debut and subsequent climb to fame were nothing short of meteoric. The release of her first album, "...Baby One More Time," after signing with Jive Records, catapulted her to international fame. Her popularity and recognition skyrocketed quickly over the world, attesting to her natural gifts and the strong emotional connection she established with her listeners. Britney, as one of the greatest pop artists of her time, forever changed the entertainment industry with her groundbreaking music videos and spectacular live shows.

CHAPTER 3

The Princess of Pop

Britney Spears has maintained her status as the Princess of Pop with a run of great albums and hit songs after the tremendous success of her debut. Her second album, Selling almost 1.3 million copies in its first week, the album debuted at No. 1 on the Billboard 200 list, the biggest launch sales ever for a female artist.

The futuristic music video for the song, in which she wore a red latex catsuit, catapulted her to stardom. Other hit songs from the album include "Lucky" and "Stronger," both of which were promoted by aesthetically spectacular music videos that attracted listeners all over the globe.

The more mature and edgy sound of Britney's third studio album, 2001's

"Britney," reflected her desire to shed her girl-next-door image in favor of a more provocative and self-assured presence. The first track, "I'm a Slave 4 U," showed a more mature and sensuous side of Britney than was previously shown in her music. Other chart-toppers on the album were "I'm Not a Girl, Not Yet a Woman" and "Overprotected," demonstrating her growing musical maturity.

In 2003, Britney released her fourth studio album, titled "In the Zone," to widespread acclaim. She got to try out new sounds with the help of some big-name producers and musicians on this record. The music video for the first song "Me Against the Music," which featured Madonna, quickly became a cultural phenomenon due to the unprecedented pairing of the two greatest names in contemporary music.

Britney Spears was unstoppable in the early 2000s, producing hit songs and albums that were heard all over the globe. Her ongoing popularity and brilliance as an artist were on full display in her ability to produce hit after hit and stay current in a brutally cutthroat market.

In the late '90s and early '00s, Britney Spears was a cultural force unlike any other. Her appearance, aesthetic, and sound became symbols of the era's popular culture. She was a groundbreaking performer who created paradigm shifts in many genres of music and film.
Britney's style was so powerful that several of her most famous costumes were immediately recognized as trends of the late '90s and early '00s. Clothing she wore in her music videos, such as the schoolgirl attire from "Baby One More Time" or the

red latex catsuit from "Oops!... I Did It Again," were immediately identifiable and were the subject of many imitators.

Beyond the realms of music and style, her influence was felt. In many ways, Britney's music videos were cultural touchstones. Videos like "Toxic" and "Slave 4 U" raised the standard for what might be accomplished in a music video with their complex choreography, novel themes, and unforgettable graphics.

There was also clear evidence of Britney's impact on newer musicians. The trajectory of her career was one that many would-be entertainers hoped to follow. A number of contemporary pop singers have named Britney Spears as an inspiration, including Katy Perry, Lady Gaga, and Selena Gomez.

As her fame and fortune grew, Britney Spears became one of the most successful female musicians of all time. Her albums often debuted at number one and sold quite well. By the year's end, she had surpassed all other female musicians in America in terms of album sales.

Britney's album and single sales have broken several records. One of the best-selling albums of all time by a young singer, her first release, "...Baby One More Time," sold over 25 million copies throughout the globe.

All three of her following albums Britney Spears made history when she became the first female artist to have four albums start at No. 1.

Her solo singles were also very highly received. Due in large part to the success of songs like "Baby One More Time

Britney's influence on the entertainment business and her musical accomplishments has garnered her a number of prizes and recognition. She is one of the most acclaimed musicians of her time since she has won several awards, including Grammys, MTV Video Music Awards, and Billboard Music Awards.

Britney Spears's crown as the "Princess of Pop" is well-earned, as she has continued to chart well with each new album and song. Her impact on the entertainment industry, particularly in the late '90s and '00s, can be seen in the way she influenced trends in music, style, and music videos. As a result of her massive success in the marketplace and widespread critical praise, she is remembered as one of the most influential people in the history of popular music.

CHAPTER 4

Personal Life and Public Image

Britney Spears, as one of the most well-known celebrities in the world, has always been subject to intense public scrutiny over her private life. Her high-profile romances and connections with other celebrities often made tabloids. In one of her first and most famous relationships, she dated fellow pop singer Justin Timberlake, whom she met on "The Mickey Mouse Club." The media gave a lot of attention to the pair during their relationship, and when they broke up in 2002, it was no different.

Britney Spears had a brief fling with dancer Kevin Federline after her breakup with Justin Timberlake. The couple were engaged in 2004 and wed in the fall of the same year. Their reality program, "Britney & Kevin: Chaotic," gave audiences an inside look at their relationship and was frequently featured in the media. However, the constant attention from the press ultimately led to the couple's separation in 2007.

The media has extensively covered Britney's following relationships, such as her 55-hour marriage to childhood buddy Jason Allen Alexander and her romance with her ex-manager, Jason Trawick. The paparazzi invaded her privacy by following her wherever she went, fueling the ongoing media frenzy over her private life.

The media's coverage of Britney Spears has had a major impact on how the public views her and how they understand the difficulties she has faced. As one of the most famous people in the world, she was constantly harassed by the paparazzi, resulting in many intrusive and frequently unpleasant news stories. Her artistic accomplishments were sometimes eclipsed by tabloid speculation about her personal life, including her romances, mental health, and parenthood.

The stresses of being a famous person affected Britney's psyche and emotional stability. Her mental health suffered as a result of the public's and media's relentless focus on her every move. Stories about her personal life in the tabloids sometimes eclipsed her musical and creative accomplishments, and her acts were frequently sensationalized.

The media's treatment of Britney Spears, in particular, reinforced negative gender norms and limiting beliefs about women's roles in show business. Her looks, fashion choices, and demeanor were often condemned, whereas the same activities on the part of male musicians were met with less backlash.

Britney Spears' mental and emotional health have been serious issues throughout her career. The stress of celebrity and the continual scrutiny from the media had an adverse effect on her psyche. Her erratic conduct and apparent mental turmoil in 2007 became the subject of much media attention.

Britney's personal problems during this time were well reported. She had to deal with the law when she briefly lost custody of her children and got into a public court fight with her parents about conservatorship. The media's preoccupation with her private life was further fueled by the sensationalized coverage of her emotional collapse.

Britney's mental health issues also necessitated therapy and professional hiatuses. To deal with her mental health and the stresses of celebrity, she checked into a clinic in 2007. The media's speculation about her illness, frequently sensationalized, only made her emotional issues worse, despite her best attempts to get assistance and take care of herself.

Britney has been frank about her struggles with mental health in recent years, sharing her experiences on social media. She has worked to raise awareness about mental health and has been an example to those going through tough times. She took a leave of absence from her job in 2019 to concentrate on her health and personal life.

The public's view of Britney Spears' difficulties with her emotional and mental health has changed throughout the years. At first, the media tended to sensationalize her problems and use them as clickbait. However, in recent years, the public and her admirers have shown more compassion and tolerance. Supporters of Britney Spears rallied behind the hashtag #FreeBritney to call for the termination of her conservatorship.

In conclusion, Britney Spears' career has been marked by intensive media scrutiny of her private life and public image. Maintaining her mental health has been difficult because of her high-profile romances, tabloid headlines, and the demands of being a celebrity. Her path and reputation have been defined by the public's knowledge of her problems with mental health. Britney Spears is still a popular figure in the music and entertainment industries because she has overcome adversity and is an advocate for mental health awareness.

CHAPTER 5

Legal and Personal Challenges

Britney Spears' connection with her parents and the ensuing conservatorship troubles have been one of the most difficult legal and emotional obstacles of her life. Jamie Spears, Britney's father, asked the court to be named her conservator in 2007 after she had a public breakdown. When an individual lacks the mental capacity to handle their own financial and personal matters, the court may appoint a conservator to do so on their behalf.

The conservatorship, which was established to aid and safeguard Britney at a time of crisis, has lasted for nearly a decade, prompting much controversy and suspicion. Fans have been vocal about their dissatisfaction with the conservatorship for some time now, starting the #FreeBritney campaign in an effort to get more freedom and independence for Britney.

Britney's father, Jamie Spears, has been the main conservator for the majority of the conservatorship arrangement, although both of Britney's parents have been involved. Lynne Spears, Britney's mother, has also been engaged in conservatorship-related legal proceedings on occasion. The public has been split on whether or not Britney's conservatorship is essential, with some believing it has limited her autonomy too much.

Due to the sensitive nature of conservatorships, little details have been shared with the public. The public's interest and worry in Britney has been piqued, however, by reports that she wants more freedom and independence in her life. She has expressed dissatisfaction with the conservatorship and its negative effects on her life, profession, and well-being throughout court proceedings.

The custody fights for Britney Spears' children have been another well known legal hurdle in her life. After Britney's 2007 divorce from Kevin Federline, the two parents had a contentious custody battle in court for their two boys, Sean Preston and Jayden James.

Britney was going through some tough times and being closely watched by the media. As a result of the court's concerns about her fitness as a parent, she lost some of her visiting privileges. The media circus that followed, with photographers continually harassing her and her family, only made matters worse.

Britney worked hard to rectify her circumstances and get custody of her children back over time. To show she was serious about becoming a good parent, the court ordered her to take a drug test and enroll in parenting programs. Her connection with her boys started to mend in earnest when she was given more visiting privileges in 2008.

Britney's relationship with her children was restored as her personal life became more stable. She has made great strides as a mother, as seen by the touching moments she has shared on social media with her boys. However, numerous tabloids have continued to use the subject for sensationalized headlines, and the public's scrutiny and suspicion about her parenting skills have remained.

Britney Spears' life and career were profoundly impacted by a public breakdown in 2007. Her mental health issues were exacerbated by the spotlight, which caused her to act erratically and suffer from depression. Her every step was chronicled by the paparazzi, resulting in intrusive and mostly unfavorable press attention.

Britney's public image degraded as a result of the intense scrutiny she faced at the time. Her mental and emotional health deteriorated due to the constant presence of the paparazzi and their relentless pursuit of dramatic headlines. She also made many contentious public appearances and shaved her head during the upheaval, which only added fuel to the media's fire.

Britney's loved ones and friends organized an intervention in early 2008, successfully convincing her to check into a treatment center. She decided to get assistance for her mental issues and get her life back on track all on her own accord. With this choice, she took the first step toward healing.

After finishing her treatment, Britney put all of her energy towards reestablishing her life and career. She made an attempt to take care of herself, going to therapy and other sources of help for her mental health issues. She came back to the music world in future years, releasing new albums and going on successful tour and a Las Vegas residency.

Britney has been open and honest about her recovery process from the beginning. She has utilized her celebrity to raise awareness about mental health concerns and combat the stigma that has long surrounded them. Her honesty and toughness have been an inspiration to many, and she has become a symbol of fortitude for others going through difficult times.

In sum, Britney Spears has had a difficult existence filled with legal and personal obstacles. The contentious nature of her relationship with her parents and the subsequent conservatorship disputes have been widely discussed and worried about. Custody fights in the courts and intense public attention just added to the difficulty of her already trying personal situation. Britney's life changed drastically after her 2007 public meltdown, which led her to treatment and ultimately sobriety. She is an inspiration to many since she has shown tenacity and a dedication to conquering problems despite so numerous setbacks.

CHAPTER 6

Resurgence and Reinvention

Britney Spears' incredible return and reinvention after a difficult period in her life and career has made her one of the most lasting and influential musicians of all time. Beginning in the late 2000s and continuing into the 2010s, she underwent a period of revitalization and reinvention that culminated in a stunning return that won the hearts of fans all over the globe.

In 2008, with the release of her sixth studio album, "Circus," Britney began her comeback. The title tune of her album served as a metaphor for her life, representing her triumphant comeback to the limelight after facing adversity. The Britney we saw in "Circus" was stronger and more self-assured, and she was clearly enjoying her newfound eedom in the spotlight.

It debuted at number one on the Billboard 200 and spawned the hits "Womanizer" and "If U Seek Amy." The later song gained notice for its racy lyrical content, demonstrating that Britney was not afraid to push musical limits and express her sexuality.

Britney's spectacular return tour kicked off during the "Circus" period. Selling out venues across the globe, Britney Spears' "Circus Starring Britney Spears" tour was lauded for her high-energy performances and lavish staging. Britney's strong stage presence and mesmerizing performances proved that she was back in full force.

Britney Spears' seventh studio album, "Femme Fatale," was released in 2011 and continued the reinvention of her sound and image that began with her triumphant return the previous year. The album showed a more sophisticated and alluring side of Britney, while still embracing the popular electro-pop style.

Collaborators on "Femme Fatale" included Max Martin, Dr. Luke, and will.i.am, to name a few of the industry's finest producers and performers. The album's main track, "Hold It Against Me," became her fourth No. 1 With the album's success riding on singles like "Till the World Ends" and "I Wanna Go," Britney cemented her reputation as a pop music powerhouse.

Britney's performances and music videos maintained their popularity throughout the

"Femme Fatale" phase. She continued to push the boundaries of performance art with each new dance routine and eye-popping music video.

Known as "Britney: Piece of Me," Britney Spears' Las Vegas residency began at The AXIS theater at Planet Hollywood Resort & Casino in 2013. The residency's original term was supposed to be short, but it has been extended many times, and is now scheduled to continue until the end of 2017.

As one of the highest-grossing and most critically acclaimed residencies in Sin City's history, "Britney: Piece of Me" shattered box office records. The show was well received by critics, who praised Britney's electric performances, lavish sets, and instantly recognizable wardrobe changes. People from all over the globe flocked to

Las Vegas to see Britney perform in her residency.

Britney's status as a cultural icon and groundbreaking performer was cemented throughout her stay. Some of her most popular songs were performed, and she also displayed her personality and artistic prowess in visually beautiful portions. She had a profound effect on the Las Vegas entertainment industry, inspiring many other A-list performers to set up permanent bases there.

Britney Spears' 2016 release of her ninth studio album, "Glory," was a watershed moment in her career. Critics regarded the album as one of her most unified and ambitious efforts due to its more experimental and mature sound.

Artistically, "Glory" demonstrated Britney's development and her openness to trying new things in her songs. The album's current sound is a result of its cooperation with modern producers and composers. The success of singles like "Make Me..." and "Slumber Party" attest to her ability to evolve her sound while staying true to her original vision.

During the "Glory" period, she also had several unforgettable performances, such as her legendary medley of classics at the 2016 MTV Video Music Awards. The concert served as a timely reminder of her everlasting impact and legacy as a music icon.

Even as Britney Spears matured as a performer, her impact on the music business and popular culture was impossible to ignore. Her influence went well beyond her famous performances and number one singles. New generations of artists found fresh motivation in her work, and many trace their own artistic development back to hers.

Britney has utilized her fame as a musician to promote a number of social concerns. She has been outspoken in her advocacy for reducing the stigma that surrounds mental health concerns. Many of her admirers have been moved to talk about mental health as a result of her willingness to be transparent about her own experiences.

The success and reinvention of Britney Spears have been nothing short of remarkable. She has shown herself to be both a cultural icon and a groundbreaking performer by bouncing back from adversity. She has maintained her popularity and the respect of her peers because to her ability to evolve with the music industry while maintaining her own unique style. Britney Spears has always been a major force in the music and entertainment industries, and that hasn't changed despite the fact that she's always reinventing herself.

THE END

Printed in the USA
CPSIA information can be obtained
at www.ICGtesting.com
LVHW011916260823
756391LV00014B/1074